Section 7 provides a pointer to some useful information on different design approaches to meeting the *energy efficiency requirements*.

1.9   In this document the following conventions have been adopted to assist understanding and interpretation:

a.   Texts shown against a green background are extracts from the Building Regulations or Building (Approved Inspectors etc.) Regulations 2000 (SI 2000/2532) ('the Approved Inspectors Regulations'), both as amended, and set out the legal requirements that relate to compliance with the *energy efficiency requirements* of building regulations. As stated previously, there is no flexibility in respect of such text; it defines a legal requirement, not guidance for typical situations. It should also be remembered that, as noted above, building works must comply with all the other applicable provisions of building regulations.

b.   Key terms are defined in paragraph 3.1 and are printed in ***bold italic text***.

c.   Details of technical publications referred to in the text of this Approved Document will be given in footnotes and repeated as references at the end of the document. A reference to a publication is likely to be made for one of two main reasons. The publication may contain additional or more comprehensive technical detail, which it would be impractical to include in full in the Approved Document but which is needed to fully explain ways of meeting the requirements; or it is a source of more general information. The reason for the reference will be indicated in each case. The reference will be to a specified edition of the document. The Approved Document may be amended from time to time to include new references or to refer to revised editions where this aids compliance.

d.   Additional *commentary in italic text* appears after some numbered paragraphs. This commentary is intended to assist understanding of the immediately preceding paragraph or sub-paragraph, or to direct readers to sources of additional information, but is not part of the technical guidance itself.

Where you can get further help

1.10   If you do not understand the technical guidance or other information set out in this Approved Document and the additional detailed technical references to which it directs you, there are a number of routes through which you can seek further assistance:

- the CLG website: www.communities.gov.uk;

- the Planning Portal website: www.planningportal.gov.uk;

- if you are the person undertaking the building work you can seek assistance either from your local authority building control service or from your approved inspector (depending on which building control service you are using);

- persons registered with a competent person self-certification scheme may be able to get technical advice from their scheme operator;

- if your query is of a highly technical nature you may wish to seek the advice of a specialist, or industry technical body, for the relevant subject.

Responsibility for compliance

1.11   It is important to remember that if you are the person (e.g. designer, builder, installer) carrying out building work to which any requirement of building regulations applies you have a responsibility to ensure that the work complies with any such requirement. The building owner may also have a responsibility for ensuring compliance with building regulation requirements and could be served with an enforcement notice in cases of non-compliance.

Section 2: The Requirements

2.1   This Approved Document, which takes effect on 1 October 2010, deals with the *energy efficiency requirements* in the Building Regulations 2000 (as amended). Regulation 2(1) of the Building Regulations defines the *energy efficiency requirements* as the requirements of regulations 4A, 17C, 17D and 17E and Part L of Schedule 1. The *energy efficiency requirements* relevant to this Approved Document, which deals with new *dwellings*, are those in regulations 17C and 17E and Part L of Schedule 1, and are set out below.

New buildings – Regulation 17C

Where a building is erected, it shall not exceed the target CO_2 emission rate for the building that has been approved pursuant to regulation 17B.

Energy performance certificates – Regulation 17E

(1) This regulation applies where—

(a) a building is erected; or

(b) a building is modified so that it has a greater or fewer number of parts designed or altered for separate use than it previously had, where the modification includes the provision or extension of any of the fixed services for heating, hot water, air conditioning or mechanical ventilation.

(2) The person carrying out the work shall—

(a) give an energy performance certificate for the building to the owner of the building; and

(b) give to the local authority notice to that effect, including the reference number under which the energy performance certificate has been registered in accordance with regulation 17F(4).

(3) The energy performance certificate and notice shall be given not later than five days after the work has been completed.

(4) The energy performance certificate must be accompanied by a recommendation report containing recommendations for the improvement of the energy performance of the building, issued by the energy assessor who issued the energy performance certificate.

(5) An energy performance certificate must—

(a) express the asset rating of the building in a way approved by the Secretary of State under regulation 17A;

(b) include a reference value such as a current legal standard or benchmark;

(c) be issued by an energy assessor who is accredited to produce energy performance certificates for that category of building; and

---

Contents

PAGE

Section 1: Introduction 2

   What is an Approved Document? 2

   Consideration of technical risk 2

   How to use this Approved Document 2

   Where you can get further help 3

   Responsibility for compliance 3

Section 2: The Requirements 4

LIMITATION ON REQUIREMENTS 6

Section 3: General guidance 7

   Key terms 7

   Types of work covered by this Approved Document 8

   Buildings that are exempt from the energy efficiency requirements 8

   Notification of work covered by the energy efficiency requirements 8

   Materials and workmanship 9

   The Workplace (Health, Safety and Welfare) Regulations 1992 9

   Demonstrating compliance 10

Section 4: Design standards 11

REGULATIONS 17A AND 17B 11

   Target CO_2 emission rate (TER) 11

   Buildings containing multiple dwellings 12

CRITERION 1 – ACHIEVING THE TER 12

   Calculating the CO_2 emissions from the actual dwelling 12

   CO_2 emission rate calculations 13

   Secondary heating 13

   Internal lighting 14

   Buildings containing multiple dwellings 14

   Achieving the target 14

CRITERION 2 – LIMITS ON DESIGN FLEXIBILITY 14

   Fabric standards 15

   System efficiencies 15

CRITERION 3 – LIMITING THE EFFECTS OF SOLAR GAINS IN SUMMER 16

Section 5: Quality of construction and commissioning 17

CRITERION 4 – BUILDING PERFORMANCE CONSISTENT WITH DER 17

   Party walls and other thermal bypasses 17

   Thermal bridges 18

   Air permeability and pressure testing 19

   Alternative to pressure testing on small developments 20

COMMISSIONING OF HEATING AND HOT WATER SYSTEMS 20

Section 6: Providing information 21

CRITERION 5 – PROVISIONS FOR ENERGY-EFFICIENT OPERATION OF THE DWELLING 21

Section 7: Model designs 22

Appendix A: Reporting evidence of compliance 23

Appendix B: Documents referred to 24

Appendix C: Standards referred to 25

Index 26

Section 1: Introduction

What is an Approved Document?

1.1 This Approved Document, which takes effect on 1 October 2010, has been approved and issued by the Secretary of State to provide practical guidance on ways of complying with the *energy efficiency requirements* (see Section 2) and regulation 7 of the Building Regulations 2000 (SI 2000/2531) for England and Wales, as amended. Regulation 2(1) of the Building Regulations defines the *energy efficiency requirements* as the requirements of regulations 4A, 17C, 17D and 17E and Part L of Schedule 1. The Building Regulations 2000 are referred to throughout the remainder of this document as 'the Building Regulations'.

1.2 The intention of issuing Approved Documents is to provide guidance about compliance with specific aspects of building regulations in some of the more common building situations. They set out what, in ordinary circumstances, may be accepted as reasonable provision for compliance with the relevant requirement(s) of building regulations to which they refer.

1.3 If guidance in an Approved Document is followed there will be a presumption of compliance with the requirement(s) covered by the guidance. However, this presumption can be overturned, so simply following guidance does not guarantee compliance; for example, if the particular case is unusual in some way, then 'normal' guidance may not be applicable. It is also important to note that there may well be other ways of achieving compliance with the requirements. **There is therefore no obligation to adopt any particular solution contained in this Approved Document if you would prefer to meet the relevant requirement in some other way. Persons intending to carry out building work should always check with their building control body, either the local authority or an approved inspector, that their proposals comply with building regulations.**

1.4 It is important to note that this Approved Document, as well as containing guidance, also contains extracts from the Regulations. Such regulatory text must be complied with as stated. For example, the requirement that the target carbon dioxide (CO_2) emission rate for the building shall not be exceeded (regulation 17C) is a regulatory requirement. There is therefore no flexibility to ignore this requirement; neither can compliance with this particular regulation be demonstrated via any route other than that set out in regulations 17A and 17B.

1.5 The guidance contained in this Approved Document relates only to the particular requirements of the Building Regulations that the document addresses (set out in Section 2). However, building work may be subject to more than one requirement of building regulations. In such cases the work will also have to comply with any other applicable requirements of building regulations.

1.6 There are Approved Documents that give guidance on each of the parts of Schedule 1 and on regulation 7. A full list of these is provided at the back of this document.

Consideration of technical risk

1.7 In relation to the construction of new *dwellings*, building work must satisfy all the technical requirements set out in regulation 17C of, and Schedule 1 to, the Building Regulations. When considering the incorporation of energy efficiency measures in *dwellings*, attention should also be paid in particular to the need to comply with Part B (fire safety), Part C (site preparation and resistance to contaminants and moisture), Part E (resistance to the passage of sound), Part F (ventilation), paragraph G3 (hot water supply and systems), Part J (combustion appliances and fuel storage systems) and Part P (electrical safety) of Schedule 1 to the Building Regulations, as well as Part L. The adoption of any particular energy efficiency measure should not involve unacceptable technical risk of, for instance, excessive condensation. Designers and builders should refer to the relevant Approved Documents and to other generally available good practice guidance to help minimise these risks.

How to use this Approved Document

1.8 This Approved Document is subdivided into seven sections as detailed below. These main sections are followed by supporting appendices.

This **introductory** section sets out the general context in which the guidance in the Approved Document must be considered.

Section 2 sets out the relevant legal requirements contained in the Building Regulations.

Section 3 contains general guidance, including the definition of key terms, the types of building work covered by this Approved Document, the types of building work that are exempt, procedures for notifying work, materials and workmanship and health and safety issues, an overview of the routes to compliance and how to deal with 'special' areas of buildings that contain *dwellings*.

Section 4 details the considerations that apply to demonstrating that the design of the *dwelling* will meet the *energy efficiency requirements*. This section begins the detailed technical guidance relating to showing compliance with the *energy efficiency requirements*.

Section 5 details the considerations that apply when demonstrating that the design has been appropriately translated into actual construction performance.

Section 6 describes the information that should be provided to occupiers to help them achieve reasonable standards of energy efficiency in practice.

Energy performance certificates – Regulation 17E *(continued)*

(d) include the following information—

(i) the reference number under which the certificate has been registered in accordance with regulation 17F(4);

(ii) the address of the building;

(iii) an estimate of the total useful floor area of the building;

(iv) the name of the energy assessor who issued it;

(v) the name and address of the energy assessor's employer, or, if he is self-employed, the name under which he trades and his address;

(vi) the date on which it was issued; and

(vii) the name of the approved accreditation scheme of which the energy assessor is a member.

(6) Certification for apartments or units designed or altered for separate use in blocks may be based—

(a) except in the case of a dwelling, on a common certification of the whole building for blocks with a common heating system; or

(b) on the assessment of another representative apartment or unit in the same block.

(7) Where —

(a) a block with a common heating system is divided into parts designed or altered for separate use; and

(b) one or more, but not all, of the parts are dwellings, certification for those parts which are not dwellings may be based on a common certification of all the parts which are not dwellings.

Requirement	*Limits on application*

Schedule 1 – Part L Conservation of fuel and power

L1. Reasonable provision shall be made for the conservation of fuel and power in buildings by:

(a) limiting heat gains and losses—

(i) through thermal elements and other parts of the building fabric; and

(ii) from pipes, ducts and vessels used for space heating, space cooling and hot water services;

(b) providing fixed building services which—

(i) are energy efficient;

(ii) have effective controls; and

(iii) are commissioned by testing and adjusting as necessary to ensure they use no more fuel and power than is reasonable in the circumstances; and

(c) providing to the owner sufficient information about the building, the fixed building services and their maintenance requirements so that the building can be operated in such a manner as to use no more fuel and power than is reasonable in the circumstances.

LIMITATION ON REQUIREMENTS

2.2   In accordance with regulation 8 of the Building Regulations, the requirements in Parts A to D, F to K and N and P (except for paragraphs G2, H2 and J6) of Schedule 1 to the Building Regulations do not require anything to be done except for the purpose of securing reasonable standards of health and safety for persons in or about buildings (and any others who may be affected by buildings or matters connected with buildings).

2.3   Paragraph G2 is excluded as it deals with water efficiency and paragraphs H2 and J6 are excluded from regulation 8 because they deal directly with prevention of the contamination of water. Parts E and M (which deal, respectively, with resistance to the passage of sound and access to and use of buildings) are excluded from regulation 8 because they address the welfare and convenience of building users. Part L is excluded from regulation 8 because it addresses the conservation of fuel and power.

Section 3: General guidance

Key terms

3.1 The following are key terms used in this document:

Air permeability is the physical property used to measure airtightness of the building fabric. It is defined as air leakage rate per hour per square metre of envelope area at a test reference pressure differential across the building envelope of 50 Pascal ($50 N/m^2$). The envelope area of the building, or measured part of the building, is the total area of all floors, walls and ceilings bordering the internal volume subject to the test. This includes walls and floors below external ground level. Overall internal dimensions are used to calculate this area and no subtractions are made for the area of the junctions of internal walls, floors and ceilings with exterior walls, floors and ceilings. The *limiting air permeability* is the worst allowable *air permeability*. The *design air permeability* is the target value set at the design stage, and must always be no worse than the limiting value. The *assessed air permeability* is the value used in establishing the *DER*, and is based on a specific measurement of the *dwelling* concerned, or on measurements of other *dwellings* of the same *dwelling type*.

The envelope area of a terraced house includes the party wall(s). The envelope area of a flat in a multiple storey building includes the floors, walls and ceilings which are shared with adjacent flats.

BCB means Building Control Body: a local authority or an approved inspector.

Commissioning means the advancement of a *fixed building service* following installation, replacement or alteration of the whole or part of the system, from the state of static completion to working order by testing and adjusting as necessary to ensure that the system as a whole uses no more fuel and power than is reasonable in the circumstances, without prejudice to the need to comply with health and safety requirements. For each system *commissioning* includes setting-to-work, regulation (that is testing and adjusting repetitively) to achieve the specified performance, the calibration, setting up and testing of the associated automatic control systems, and recording of the system settings and the performance test results that have been accepted as satisfactory.

Controlled service or fitting means a service or fitting in relation to which Part G (sanitation, hot water safety and water efficiency), H (drainage and waste disposal), J (combustion appliances and fuel storage systems), L (conservation of fuel and power) or P (electrical safety) of Schedule 1 to the Building Regulations imposes a requirement.

DER is the *Dwelling* CO_2 Emission Rate expressed as $kgCO_2/(m^2.year)$.

Dwelling means a self-contained unit designed to accommodate a single household. Buildings exclusively containing **rooms for residential purposes** such as nursing homes, student accommodation and similar are not **dwellings**, and in such cases, Approved Document L2A applies.

Dwelling type is a means of allocating each *dwelling* on a development to a particular group to provide the basis for assessing the pressure testing regime. The allocation of each *dwelling* to a *dwelling type* should be the responsibility of the person carrying out the pressure testing. To be classed as of the same type *dwellings* have to:

i.   be of the same generic form (i.e. detached, semi-detached, end terrace, mid-terrace, ground-floor flat (inc. ground-floor maisonette), mid-floor flat, top-floor flat (inc. top-floor maisonette);

ii. be of the same number of storeys;

iii. be of the same *design air permeability*;

iv. have similar adjacency to unheated spaces such as stairwells, integral garages, etc.

v.   have the same principal construction details (as identified by the Accredited Construction Details (ACD) or bespoke detail reference codes);

vi. have a similar (i.e. ±1) number of significant penetrations, i.e. for windows, doors, flues/chimneys, supply/exhaust terminals, waste water pipes;

vii. have envelope areas that do not differ by more than 10 per cent (see *air permeability* for a definition of envelope area).

Energy efficiency requirements means the requirements of regulations 4A, 17C, 17D and 17E of, and Part L of Schedule 1 to, the Building Regulations.

Fixed building services means any part of, or any controls associated with:

a. fixed internal or external lighting systems, but does not include emergency escape lighting or specialist process lighting; or

b. fixed systems for heating, hot water, air-conditioning or mechanical ventilation.

Room for residential purposes means a room, or a suite of rooms, which is not a dwelling-house or a flat and which is used by one or more persons to live and sleep in and includes a room in a hostel, a hotel, a boarding house, a hall of residence or a residential home, whether or not the room is separated from or arranged in a cluster group with other rooms, but does not include a room in a hospital, or other similar establishment, used for patient accommodation and, for the purposes of this definition, a 'cluster' is a group of rooms for residential purposes which is:

a. separated from the rest of the building in which it is situated by a door which is designed to be locked; and

b. not designed to be occupied by a single household.

TER is the Target CO_2 Emission Rate expressed as $kgCO_2/(m^2.year)$ (see paragraphs 4.2 to 4.6).

Types of work covered by this Approved Document

3.2   This Approved Document is intended to give guidance on what, in ordinary circumstances, may be considered reasonable provision for compliance with the requirements of regulation 17C of, and Part L of Schedule 1 to, the Building Regulations for those creating new *dwellings*. In addition it gives guidance on compliance with regulations 20B, 20C and 20D of the Building Regulations and 12B, 12C and 12D of the Approved Inspectors Regulations.

Live-work units

3.3   If a unit contains both living accommodation and space to be used for commercial purposes (e.g. workshop or office), the whole unit should be treated as a *dwelling* as long as the commercial part could revert to domestic use. This could be the case if, for example:

a. there is direct access between the commercial space and the living accommodation; and

b. both are contained within the same thermal envelope; and

c. the living accommodation occupies a substantial proportion of the total area of the unit.

Sub-paragraph c means that the presence of (e.g.) a small manager's flat in a large non-domestic building would not result in the whole building being treated as a dwelling. Similarly, the existence of a room used as an office or utility space within a dwelling would not mean that the building should not be treated as a dwelling.

Mixed-use developments

3.4   When constructing a *dwelling* as part of a larger building that contains other types of accommodation, sometimes called a mixed-use development, this Approved Document L1A should be used for guidance in relation to each individual *dwelling*. Approved Document L2A gives guidance relating to the non-dwelling parts of such buildings such as heated common areas, and in the case of mixed-use developments, the commercial or retail space.

Material changes of use

3.5   The erection of a new *dwelling* is not a material change of use. Approved Document L1B applies where a *dwelling* is being created in an existing building as the result of a material change of use of all or part of the building.

Buildings that are exempt from the energy efficiency requirements

3.6   No new *dwellings* are exempt from the *energy efficiency requirements* of the Building Regulations.

Notification of work covered by the energy efficiency requirements

3.7   In all cases where it is proposed to erect a new *dwelling* building regulations require the person proposing to carry out the work to notify a *BCB* in advance of any work starting. This notification would usually be by way of full plans (or possibly a building notice) given to a local authority, or an initial notice given jointly with the approved inspector. However, some elements of the work may not need to be notified to a *BCB* in advance, as set out in paragraphs 3.8 to 3.11 below.

Competent person self-certification schemes

3.8   It is not necessary to notify a *BCB* in advance of work which is to be carried out by a person registered with a relevant competent person self-certification scheme listed in Schedule 2A to the Building Regulations. In order to join such a scheme a person must demonstrate competence to carry out the type of work the scheme covers, and also the ability to comply with all relevant requirements in the Building Regulations.

3.9   Where work is carried out by a person registered with a competent person scheme, regulation 16A of the Building Regulations 2000 and regulation 11A of the Building (Approved Inspectors etc) Regulations 2000 require that the occupier of the building be given, within 30 days of the completion of the work, a certificate confirming that the work complies fully with all applicable building regulation requirements. There is also a requirement to give the *BCB* a notice of the work carried out, again within 30 days of the completion of the work. These certificates and notices are usually made available through the scheme operator.

3.10   *BCBs* are authorised to accept these certificates and notices as evidence of compliance with the requirements of the Building Regulations. Local authority inspection and enforcement powers remain unaffected, although they are normally used only in response to a complaint that work does not comply.

3.11   There are no competent person schemes which cover all aspects of the construction of a new *dwelling*. There are, however, schemes which cover the electrical and plumbing installation work and the installation of certain *fixed building services* (heating, hot water, air-conditioning, mechanical ventilation).

3.12   A list of competent person self-certification schemes and the types of work for which they are authorised can be found at www.communities.gov.uk

Materials and workmanship

3.13   Any building work which is subject to the requirements imposed by Schedule 1 to the Building Regulations should, in accordance with regulation 7, be carried out with proper materials and in a workmanlike manner.

3.14   You may show that you have complied with regulation 7 in a number of ways. These include demonstrating the appropriate use of:

- a product bearing CE marking in accordance with the Construction Products Directive (89/106/EEC)[1], as amended by the CE Marking Directive (93/68/EC)[2], the Low Voltage Directive (2006/95/EC)[3] and the EMC Directive (2004/108/EC)[4];

- a product complying with an appropriate technical specification (as defined in those Directives mentioned above), a British Standard, or an alternative national technical specification of a Member State of the European Union or Turkey[5], or of another State signatory to the Agreement on the European Economic Area (EEA) that provides an equivalent level of safety and protection;

- a product covered by a national or European certificate issued by a European Technical Approval Issuing body, provided the conditions of use are in accordance with the terms of the certificate.

3.15   You will find further guidance in the Approved Document which specifically supports regulation 7 on materials and workmanship.

Independent certification schemes

3.16   There are many UK product certification schemes. Such schemes certify compliance with the requirements of a recognised standard that is appropriate to the purpose for which the material is to be used. Materials which are not so certified may still conform to a relevant standard.

3.17   Many certification bodies that approve products under such schemes are accredited by the United Kingdom Accreditation Service (UKAS). Such bodies can issue certificates only for the categories of product covered under the terms of their accreditation.

3.18   *BCBs* may take into account the certification of products, components, materials or structures under such schemes as evidence of compliance with the relevant standard. Similarly, *BCBs* may accept the certification of the installation or maintenance of products, components, materials or structures under such schemes as evidence of

compliance with the relevant standard. Nonetheless, before accepting that certification constitutes compliance with building regulations, a *BCB* should establish in advance that the relevant scheme is adequate for that purpose.

Standards and technical specifications

3.19   Building regulations are made for specific purposes, including securing the health, safety, welfare and convenience of people in or about buildings; furthering the conservation of fuel and power; furthering the protection or enhancement of the environment; and facilitating sustainable development. Guidance contained in standards and technical approvals referred to in Approved Documents may be relevant to compliance with building regulations to the extent that it relates to those purposes. However, it should be noted that guidance in standards and technical approvals may also address other aspects of performance such as serviceability, or aspects which, although they relate to health and safety, are not covered by building regulations.

3.20   When an Approved Document makes reference to a named standard or document, the relevant version of the standard or document is the one listed at the end of the Approved Document. Until the reference in the Approved Document is revised, the standard or document listed remains the approved source, but if the issuing body has published a revised or updated version, any content that addresses the relevant requirements of the Building Regulations may be used as a source of guidance.

3.21   The appropriate use of a product in compliance with a European Technical Approval as defined in the Construction Products Directive will meet the relevant requirements.

3.22   Communities and Local Government intends to issue periodic amendments to its Approved Documents to reflect emerging harmonised European standards. Where a national standard is to be replaced by a European harmonised standard, there will be a coexistence period during which either standard may be referred to. At the end of the coexistence period the national standard will be withdrawn.

The Workplace (Health, Safety and Welfare) Regulations 1992

3.23   The Workplace (Health, Safety and Welfare) Regulations 1992, as amended, apply to the common parts of flats and similar buildings if people such as cleaners, wardens and caretakers are employed to work in these common parts. These Regulations contain some requirements which affect building design. The main requirements are now covered by the Building Regulations, but for further information see *Workplace health, safety and welfare, Workplace (Health, Safety and Welfare) Regulations 1992, Approved Code of Practice and guidance*, HSE publication L24, HMSO, 1996.

---

[1]   As implemented by the Construction Products Regulations 1991 (SI 1991/1620).
[2]   As implemented by the Construction Products (Amendment) Regulations 1994 (SI 1994/3051).
[3]   As implemented by the Electrical Equipment (Safety) Regulations 1994 (SI 1994/3260).
[4]   As implemented by the Electromagnetic Compatibility Regulations 2006 (SI 2006/3418).
[5]   Decision No 1/95 of the EC-Turkey Association Council of 22 December 1995.

Demonstrating compliance

3.24   In the Secretary of State's view, compliance with the **energy efficiency requirements** could be demonstrated by meeting all five criteria set out in the following paragraphs. It is expected that software implementations of SAP 2009 will produce an output report that will assist **BCBs** to check that compliance has been achieved.

*The output report can benefit both developers and **BCBs** during the design and construction stages as well as at completion.*

3.25   Criterion 1: in accordance with regulation 17C, the calculated rate of CO_2 emissions from the **dwelling** (the Dwelling Emission Rate, **DER**) must not be greater than the Target Emission Rate (**TER**), which is determined by following the procedure set out in paragraphs 4.7 to 4.17.

Criterion 1 is a regulation and is therefore mandatory, whereas Criteria 2 to 5 are only guidance. The calculations required as part of the procedure used to show compliance with this criterion can also provide information needed to prepare the Energy Performance Certificate required by regulation 17E of the Building Regulations and by the Energy Performance of Buildings (Certificates and Inspections) (England and Wales) Regulations 2007 (SI 2007/991) as amended.

3.26   Criterion 2: the performance of the building fabric and the **fixed building services** should achieve reasonable overall standards of energy efficiency following the procedure set out in paragraphs 4.18 to 4.24.

This is intended to place limits on design flexibility to discourage excessive and inappropriate trade-offs – e.g. buildings with poor insulation standards offset by renewable energy systems with uncertain service lives. This emphasises the purpose of Criterion 2.

3.27   Criterion 3: the **dwelling** should have appropriate passive control measures to limit the effect of solar gains on indoor temperatures in summer, irrespective of whether or not the **dwelling** has mechanical cooling. The guidance given in paragraphs 4.25 to 4.27 of this Approved Document provides a way of demonstrating that reasonable provision has been made.

*The aim is to counter excessive internal temperature rise in summer to reduce or eliminate the need for air conditioners. Criterion 3 should be satisfied even if the **dwelling** is air conditioned.*

3.28   Criterion 4: the performance of the **dwelling**, as built, should be consistent with the **DER**. The guidance in Section 5 should be used to demonstrate that this criterion has been met. Extra credits will be given in the **TER/DER** calculation where builders provide robust evidence of quality-assured procedures in the design and construction phases.

3.29   Criterion 5: the necessary provisions for energy efficient operation of the **dwelling** should be put in place. One way to achieve this would be by following the guidance in Section 6.

'Special areas' related to dwellings

3.30   The following paragraphs describe some 'special areas' that fall outside the normal five criteria, and give guidance on how reasonable provision for the conservation of fuel and power can be demonstrated.

Common areas in buildings with multiple dwellings

3.31   The common areas of buildings containing more than one **dwelling** are not classified as **dwellings**, and therefore fall outside the scope of the five criteria outlined above. For such areas, reasonable provision would be:

a. if they are heated, to follow the guidance in Approved Document L2A; or

b. if they are unheated, to provide fabric elements that meet the fabric standards set out in paragraphs 4.20 to 4.22.

Conservatories and porches

3.32   Where conservatories and porches are installed at the same time as the construction of a new **dwelling**, the guidance in this document applies. For conservatories and porches added as extensions to a **dwelling**, see guidance in Approved Document L1B.

Swimming pool basins

3.33   Where a swimming pool is constructed as part of a new **dwelling**, reasonable provision should be made to limit heat loss from the pool basin by achieving a U-value no worse than 0.25 $W/m^2.K$ as calculated according to BS EN ISO 13370[6].

3.34   In terms of Criterion 1, the **dwelling** should be assessed as if the pool basin were not there, although the pool hall should be included. The area covered by the pool should be replaced with the equivalent area of floor with the same U-value as the pool surround.

---

[6]   BS EN ISO 13370 Thermal performance of buildings. Heat transfer via the ground. Calculation methods.

Section 4: Design standards

REGULATIONS 17A AND 17B

4.1 Regulations 17A, 17B and 17C of the Building Regulations implement Articles 3, 4 and 5 of the Energy Performance of Buildings Directive. Regulations 17A and 17B state that:

Methodology of calculation of the energy performance of buildings

17A.–(1) The Secretary of State shall approve–

a. a methodology of calculation of the energy performance of buildings, including methods for calculating asset ratings and operational ratings of buildings; and

b. ways in which the energy performance of buildings, as calculated in accordance with the methodology, shall be expressed.

(2) In this regulation–

'asset rating' means a numerical indicator of the amount of energy estimated to meet the different needs associated with a standardised use of the building; and

'operational rating' means a numerical indicator of the amount of energy consumed during the occupation of the building over a period of time.

Minimum energy performance requirements for buildings

17B.–The Secretary of State shall approve minimum energy performance requirements for new buildings, in the form of target CO_2 emission rates, which shall be based upon the methodology approved pursuant to regulation 17A.

Target CO_2 Emission Rate (*TER*)

4.2 The Target CO_2 Emission Rate (*TER*) is the minimum energy performance requirement for a new *dwelling* approved by the Secretary of State in accordance with regulation 17B. It is expressed in terms of the mass of CO_2, in units of kg per m² of floor area per year, emitted as a result of the provision of the specified *fixed building services* for a standardised household when assessed using approved calculation tools.

4.3 In accordance with the methodology approved by the Secretary of State in the Notice of Approval[7], the *TER* for individual *dwellings* must be calculated using SAP 2009.

4.4 The *TER* is calculated in two stages:

a. First calculate the CO_2 emissions from a 2002 notional *dwelling* of the same size and shape as the actual *dwelling* and which is constructed according to the reference values set out in Appendix R of SAP 2009. No values may be

varied from these reference values when establishing the *TER*. The calculation tool will report the CO_2 emissions (based on SAP2005 CO_2 emission factors) arising from:

i. The provision of space heating and hot water (which includes the energy used by pumps and fans), C_H

ii. The use of internal lighting, C_L

b. Secondly, calculate the 2010 *TER* using the following formula:

$$TER_{2010} = (C_H \times FF \times EFA_H + C_L \times EFA_L) \times (1 - 0.2) \times (1 - 0.25)$$

Where FF is the fuel factor[8] taken from Table 1 in accordance with the guidance in paragraph 4.5.

Where EFA is the Emission Factor Adjustment with separate values for heating and lighting. EFA is the ratio of the CO_2 emission factor for the relevant fuel at 2010 divided by the value used in the 2006 edition of Part L (see table 12 of SAP 2009 and table 12 of SAP 2005 for the relevant values). For those fuels with a fuel factor of 1.0, the EFA should always be based upon mains gas.

*Note that the notional **dwelling** used to determine C_H has a party wall heat loss of zero. This means that the targeted improvement of 25 per cent is in addition to treating the party wall loss (see paragraphs 5.3 to 5.8).*

4.5 The fuel to be used for determining the fuel factor from Table 1 is one of those used to provide heating and hot water to the actual *dwelling* as follows:

a. Where all the space heating and domestic hot water heating appliances are served by the same fuel, the fuel used in those appliances.

b. Where the *dwelling* has more than one appliance for space heating and/or domestic hot water and these are served by different fuels,

i. mains gas if any of the appliances are fired by mains gas,

ii. otherwise the fuel used for the main space heating system.

c. Where the *dwelling* is served by a community heating scheme,

i. mains gas if the community scheme used mains gas for any purpose,

ii. otherwise the fuel that provides the most heat for the community scheme.

---

[7] Notice of Approval of the methodology of calculation of the energy performance of buildings in England and Wales.

[8] The fuel factor is the greater of 1.0 and the square root of the ratio of the CO_2 emission factor for the fuel to the emission factor for mains gas (both taken from table 12 of SAP 2005) rounded to two decimal places.

Table 1 Fuel factor

Heating fuel	Fuel factor[1]
Mains gas	1.00
LPG	1.10
Oil	1.17
B30K	1.00
Grid electricity for direct acting and storage systems	1.47
Grid electricity for heat pumps[2]	1.47
Solid mineral fuel[3]	1.28
Any fuel with a CO_2 emission factor less than that of mains gas	1.00
Solid multi-fuel[3]	1.00

Notes:

1. The fuel factors in Table 1 will be kept under review as progress is made towards the zero carbon target.

2. The fuel factor for electric heat pumps will be reviewed after the renewable heat incentive is introduced.

3. The specific fuel factor should be used for those appliances that can only burn the particular fuel. Where an appliance is classed as multi-fuel, the multi-fuel factor should be used except where the dwelling is in a Smoke Control Area. In such cases the solid mineral fuel figure should be used, unless the specific appliance type has been approved for use within Smoke Control Areas.

Buildings containing multiple dwellings

4.6 Where a building contains more than one *dwelling* (such as in a terrace of houses or in a block of flats), an average *TER* can be calculated for all the *dwellings* in the building. In such cases, the average *TER* is the floor-area-weighted average of all the individual *TERs*, and is calculated according to the following formula:

$$\{(\textbf{\textit{TER}}_1 \times \text{Floor area}_1) + (\textbf{\textit{TER}}_2 \times \text{Floor area}_2) + (\textbf{\textit{TER}}_3 \times \text{Floor area}_3) + ...)\} \div \{(\text{Floor area}_1 + \text{Floor area}_2 + \text{Floor area}_3) + ...\}$$

Block averaging is only permitted for multiple *dwellings* in the same building. It is not permitted across multiple buildings on the same development site.

CRITERION 1 – ACHIEVING THE *TER*

4.7 Regulation 17C states that:

New buildings – Regulation 17C

Where a building is erected, it shall not exceed the target CO_2 emission rate for the building that has been approved pursuant to regulation 17B.

Calculating the CO_2 emissions from the actual dwelling

4.8 To comply with regulation 17C, the *DER* must be no worse than the *TER* calculated as set out in paragraphs 4.2 to 4.6. The final *DER* calculation produced in accordance with regulation 20D (see paragraph 4.11 below) must be based on the building as constructed, incorporating:

a. any changes to the list of specifications that have been made during construction; and

b. the *assessed air permeability*. The *assessed air permeability* shall be determined as follows:

   i. where the *dwelling* has been pressure tested, the *assessed air permeability* is the measured *air permeability*;

   ii. where the *dwelling* has not been tested, the *assessed air permeability* is the average test result obtained from other *dwellings* of the same *dwelling type* on the development increased by a margin of +2.0 $m^3/(h.m^2)$ at 50 Pa;

   iii. on small developments (see paragraph 5.23), where the builder has opted to avoid testing, the *assessed air permeability* is the value of 15 $m^3/(h.m^2)$ at 50 Pa.

Note that builders can test a greater proportion of their dwellings and take credit for the increased robustness of the data, compared to option ii), where the assessed air permeability is taken as the average of other test results plus a safety margin. This margin has been taken as approximately one standard deviation as derived from the analysis of a large sample of data from post-2006 dwellings. The outcome of this change is that the design air permeability should be at most 8.0 $m^3/(h.m^2)$ at 50 Pa, so that untested dwellings should achieve an assessed air permeability less than the limiting value of 10 $m^3/(h.m^2)$ at 50 Pa. If the design is aiming to achieve a low design air permeability, then the margin added under paragraph ii will have a significant impact on the calculated DER. In such cases, the builder should consider testing the dwelling so that the measured permeability can be included in the calculation.

CO_2 emission rate calculations

4.9   Regulation 20D[9] states:

20D.–(1) This regulation applies where a building is erected and regulation 17C applies.

(2) Not later than the day before the work starts, the person carrying out the work shall give the local authority a notice which specifies–

a.   the target CO_2 emission rate for the building,

b.   the calculated CO_2 emission rate for the building as designed, and

c.   a list of specifications to which the building is to be constructed.

(3) Not later than five days after the work has been completed, the person carrying out the work shall give the local authority–

a.   a notice which specifies–

   i.   the target CO_2 emission rate for the building,

   ii.   the calculated CO_2 emission rate for the building as constructed, and

   iii. whether the building has been constructed in accordance with the list of specifications referred to in paragraph (2) (c), and if not a list of any changes to those specifications; or

b.   a certificate of the sort referred to in paragraph (4) accompanied by the information referred to in sub-paragraph (a).

(4) A local authority is authorised to accept, as evidence that the requirements of regulation 17C have been satisfied, a certificate to that effect by an energy assessor who is accredited to produce such certificates for that category of building.

(5) In this regulation–

'energy assessor' means an individual who is a member of an accreditation scheme approved by the Secretary of State in accordance with regulation 17F; and

'specifications' means specifications used for the calculation of the CO_2 emission rate.

CO_2 emission rate calculation *before commencement of work*

4.10   As required by regulations 17C and 20D, before the work starts, the builder shall carry out a calculation that demonstrates that the **DER** of the **dwelling** as-designed is not greater than the **TER**. This design-based calculation shall be provided to the **BCB**, along with a list of specifications used in calculating the **DER.**

*This design stage calculation and provision of a list of specifications will assist the **BCB** to confirm that what is being built aligns with the claimed performance. As set out at Appendix A, it is expected that software implementations of SAP2009 will be used to produce the list of specifications and highlight those features of the design that are critical to achieving compliance. These 'key features' can be used to prioritise the risk-based inspection of the **dwelling** as part of confirming compliance with Regulation 17C. If a provisional energy rating is calculated at this stage and an interim recommendations report is therefore available, the recommendations should be reviewed by the developer to see if further carbon mitigation measures might be incorporated in a cost effective manner.*

CO_2 emission rate calculation *after completion*

4.11   After work has been completed, the builder must notify the **BCB** of the **TER** and **DER** and whether the building has been constructed in accordance with the list of specifications submitted to the **BCB** before work started. If not, a list of any changes to the design-stage list of specifications must be given to the **BCB**. **BCB**s are authorised to accept, as evidence of compliance, a certificate to this effect signed off by a suitably accredited energy assessor.

*It would be useful to provide additional information to support the values used in the **DER** calculation and the list of specifications. For example, U-values might be determined from a specific calculation, in which case the details should be provided, or from an accredited source, in which case a reference to that source would be sufficient. For example, for a boiler, the model reference and fuel type is sufficient evidence to allow the claimed performance to be checked against the SEDBUK (Seasonal Efficiencies of Domestic Boilers in the UK) database. It would also be useful if evidence was provided that demonstrates that the **dwelling** as designed satisfies the requirements of Criteria 2 and 3.*

Secondary heating

4.12   A secondary heating appliance may meet part of the space heat demand. When calculating the **DER**, the fraction provided by the secondary heating system must be as defined by SAP 2009 for the particular combination of main heating system and secondary heating appliance. The following secondary heating appliance must be used when calculating the **DER**:

a.   Where a secondary heating appliance is fitted, the efficiency of the actual appliance with its appropriate fuel must be used in the calculation of the **DER**;

---

[9]   There is a similar regulation (Regulation 12D) in the Building (Approved Inspectors etc.) Regulations 2000 (SI 2000/2532) which applies when an approved inspector is the BCB.

b. Where a chimney or flue is provided but no appliance is actually installed, then the presence of the following appliances shall be assumed when calculating the *DER*:

   i. if a gas point is located adjacent to the hearth, a decorative fuel effect gas fire open to the chimney or flue with an efficiency of 20 per cent;

   ii. if there is no gas point, an open fire in grate for burning multi-fuel with an efficiency of 37 per cent, unless the *dwelling* is in a smoke control area when the fuel should be taken as smokeless solid mineral fuel;

c. Otherwise it shall be assumed that the secondary heating system has the same efficiency as the main heating system and is served by the same fuel, i.e. the equivalent of having no secondary heating system.

Internal lighting

4.13 In all cases the *DER* shall be calculated assuming the proportion of low-energy lamps as actually installed in the fixed lighting locations.

This means that low-energy lighting provision is tradable. The minimum amount that would be reasonable provision in the actual building is given in the Domestic Building Services Compliance Guide.

Buildings containing multiple dwellings

4.14 Where a building contains more than one *dwelling* (such as in a terrace of houses or in a block of flats), compliance with regulation 17C is achieved if:

a. EITHER every individual *dwelling* has a *DER* that is no greater than its corresponding *TER*;

b. OR the average *DER* is no greater than the average *TER*. The average *DER* is the floor-area-weighted average of all the individual *DERs*, and is calculated in the same way as the average *TER*. Block averaging is permitted only across multiple *dwellings* in a single building, NOT across multiple buildings on a development site (see paragraph 4.6).

When adopting the average DER approach, it will still be necessary to provide information for each individual dwelling, as required by regulation 20D.

Achieving the target

4.15 Provided the *dwelling* satisfies the limits on design flexibility as set out in Criterion 2, the compliance procedure allows the designer full flexibility to achieve the *TER* utilising fabric and system measures and the integration of low and zero carbon (LZC) technologies in whatever mix is appropriate to the scheme. The approved compliance tools include appropriate algorithms that enable the designer to assess the role

LZC technologies (including local renewable and low-carbon schemes driven by planning requirements[10]) can play in achieving the *TER*.

4.16 Where a *dwelling* is connected to a community energy system, the same percentage reduction in emissions should be attributed to each connected *dwelling*, and the submission should demonstrate that the capacity of the community scheme is sufficient to provide the percentage that is assumed.

4.17 In order to facilitate incorporation of improvements in system efficiencies and the integration with low and zero carbon technologies, the designer should:

a. consider adopting heating system designs that use low distribution temperatures; and

b. where multiple systems serve the same end use, organise the control strategies such that priority is given to the least carbon-intensive option; and

For example, where a solar hot water system is available, the controls should be arranged so that the best use is made of the available solar energy.

c. consider making the *dwelling* easily adaptable by facilitating the integration of additional low and zero carbon technologies at a later date. Providing appropriate facilities at the construction stage can make subsequent enhancements much easier and cheaper, e.g. providing capped off connections that can link into a planned community heating scheme.

CRITERION 2 – LIMITS ON DESIGN FLEXIBILITY

4.18 While the approach to complying with Criterion 1 allows considerable design flexibility, paragraph L1(a)(i) of Schedule 1 to the Building Regulations requires that reasonable provision should be made to limit heat gains and losses through the fabric of the building, and paragraphs L1(b)(i) and (ii) require that energy-efficient *fixed building services* with effective controls should be provided.

4.19 One way of showing that the requirement has been satisfied would be to demonstrate that the fabric elements and the *fixed building services* all satisfy the minimum energy efficiency standards specified in the following paragraphs.

Note that in order to satisfy the TER, the building specification will need to be considerably better than the stated values in many aspects of the design.

---

[10] See the Planning Policy Statement Planning and climate change and its supporting practice guidance at: www.communities.gov.uk/planningandbuilding/planning/planningpolicyguidance/planningpolicystatements/planningpolicystatements/ppsclimatechange/

Fabric standards

4.20   Table 2 sets out the worst acceptable standards for fabric properties. The stated value represents the area-weighted average value for all elements of that type. In general, the achievement of the *TER* is likely to require significantly better fabric performance than is set out in Table 2.

4.21   U-values shall be calculated using the methods and conventions set out in BR 443[11], and should be based on the whole element or unit (e.g. in the case of a window, the combined performance of the glazing and the frame).

In the case of windows, the U-value can be taken as that for:

a.   the smaller of the two standard windows defined in BS EN 14351-1[12]; or

b.   the standard configuration set out in BR 443; or

c.   the specific size and configuration of the actual window.

For domestic-type construction, SAP 2009 Table 6e gives values for different window configurations that can be used in the absence of test data or calculated values.

4.22   The U-values for roof windows and rooflights given in this Approved Document are based on the U-value having been assessed with the roof window or rooflight in the vertical position. If a particular unit has been assessed in a plane other than the vertical, the standards given in this Approved Document should be modified by making an adjustment that is dependent on the slope of the unit following the guidance given in BR 443.

System efficiencies

4.23   Each *fixed building service* should be at least as efficient as the worst acceptable value for the particular type of appliance as set out in the *Domestic Building Services Compliance Guide*[13]. If the type of appliance is not covered by the Guide, then reasonable provision would be to demonstrate that the proposed system is not less efficient than a comparable system that is covered by the Guide.

To not inhibit innovation.

4.24   The efficiency claimed for the *fixed building service* should be based on the appropriate test standard as set out in the Guide and the test data should be certified by a notified body. It would be reasonable for *BCBs* to accept such data at face value. In the absence of such quality assured data, the *BCB* should satisfy itself that the claimed performance is justified.

Table 2 Limiting fabric parameters

Roof	0.20 W/m².K
Wall	0.30 W/m².K
Floor	0.25 W/m².K
Party wall	0.20 W/m².K
Windows, roof windows, glazed rooflights, curtain walling and pedestrian doors	2.00 W/m².K
Air permeability	10.00 m³/h.m² at 50 Pa

Approved Document C gives limiting values for individual elements to minimise condensation risk.

---

[11]   BR 443 Conventions for U-value calculations, BRE, 2006.
[12]   EN 14351-1, *Windows and doors – Product standard, performance characteristics*, 2006.

[13]   Domestic Building Services Compliance Guide, CLG, 2010 Edition.

CRITERION 3 – LIMITING THE EFFECTS OF SOLAR GAINS IN SUMMER

4.25   As required by paragraph L1(a)(i) of Schedule 1 to the Building Regulations, reasonable provision should be made to limit solar gains. Solar gains are beneficial in winter as a means of offsetting heating demand, but can contribute to overheating in the summer months. Limiting the effects of solar gain in summer can be achieved by an appropriate combination of window size and orientation, solar protection through shading and other solar control measures, ventilation (day and night) and high thermal capacity. If ventilation is provided using a balanced mechanical system, consideration should be given to providing a summer bypass function during warm weather (or allow the **dwelling** to operate via natural ventilation) so that the ventilation is more effective in reducing overheating.

4.26   SAP 2009 Appendix P contains a procedure enabling designers to check whether solar gains are excessive. Reasonable provision would be achieved if the SAP assessment indicates that the **dwelling** will not have a high risk of high internal temperatures. This assessment should be done regardless of whether or not the **dwelling** has mechanical cooling. If the **dwelling** has mechanical cooling, the assessment should be based on the design without the cooling system operating, but with an appropriate assumption about effective air change rate through openable windows.

Designers may wish to go beyond the requirements in the current Building Regulations to consider the impacts of future global warming on the risks of higher internal temperatures occurring more often. CIBSE TM 36 Climate change and the indoor environment[14] gives guidance on this issue.

4.27   When seeking to limit solar gains, consideration should be given to the provision of adequate levels of daylight. BS 8206 – 2 Code of practice for daylighting[15] gives guidance on maintaining adequate levels of daylight.

*The Building Regulations do not specify minimum daylight requirements. However, reducing window area produces conflicting impacts on the predicted CO_2 emissions: reduced solar gain but increased use of electric lighting. As a general guide, if the area of glazing is much less than 20 per cent of the total floor area, some parts of the **dwelling** may experience poor levels of daylight, resulting in increased use of electric lighting.*

---

[14]   TM36 Climate change and the indoor environment: impacts and adaptation, CIBSE, 2005.
[15]   BS 8206–2:2008 Lighting for buildings. Code of practice for daylighting.

Section 5: Quality of construction and commissioning

CRITERION 4 – BUILDING PERFORMANCE CONSISTENT WITH *DER*

5.1 *Dwellings* should be constructed and equipped so that performance is consistent with the calculated *DER*. As indicated in paragraph 4.8, a final calculation of the *DER* is required to take account of any changes in performance between design and construction and to demonstrate that the building as constructed meets the *TER* as required by regulation 17C. The following paragraphs in this section set out what in normal circumstances would be reasonable provision to ensure that the actual performance of the building is consistent with the *DER*.

The provision of information referred to in paragraph 4.10 will assist BCBs in checking that the key features of the design are included during the construction process.

5.2 In accordance with Part L and regulation 7, the building fabric should be constructed to a reasonable standard so that:

a. the insulation is reasonably continuous over the whole building envelope; and

b. the *air permeability* is within reasonable limits.

Party walls and other thermal bypasses

5.3 Contrary to previous assumptions, party cavity-walls may not be zero heat loss walls because air flow in the cavity provides a heat loss mechanism.

Where outside air is able to flow into the party wall cavity a cold zone is created which results in heat flux through the wall sections on either side. The extent of air flow and heat flux will depend on external conditions such as wind and temperatures and also on the setting up of a ventilation stack effect caused by the warmed air rising in the cavity to be replaced by cooler air drawn in from outside. The air movements involved can be significant and, if no steps are taken to restrict flows, the resulting heat losses can be large.

5.4 The heat loss can be reduced by measures that restrict air movement through the cavity, either by means of fully filling the cavity and/or by providing effective sealing around the perimeter. Generic solutions to minimising party wall heat loss are available at www.planningportal.gov.uk. The extent to which heat loss can be reduced will be dependent on the detailed design and the quality of construction. In the absence of any specific, independent scientific field evidence, reasonable provision would be to adopt the guidance on U-values in paragraph 5.5.

Fully filling the cavity may have implications for sound transmission through party walls. Developers who follow this route must satisfy the BCB that the requirements of Part E will be satisfied, either by adopting a full fill detail accredited under the Robust Details scheme, or through specific site testing.

5.5 In calculating the *DER* for a *dwelling*, the party wall U-value to be assumed for the type of construction adopted is set out in Table 3.

5.6 In applying the U-values in Table 3 it is important that where edge sealing is adopted, either on its own or in conjunction with a fully filled cavity, the sealing is effective in restricting air flow and is aligned with the thermal envelope. Although effective sealing may be part of a cavity barrier which is provided in order to comply with Part B (Fire), a cavity barrier on its own may not be effective in restricting air flow. In order to claim a reduced U-value (0.2 or 0.0) it will be necessary to demonstrate that the design adopted is likely to be robust under normal site conditions. In addition, it is important that the sealing system be applied in such a way as to be in line with the thermal envelope. Any solution to reducing party wall heat loss must take into account all the requirements in Schedule 1, but particular attention should be given to the requirements of Part E.

For example, in a room-in-roof design, the insulation layer may follow the sloping roof sections to a horizontal ceiling then continue at ceiling level. In such a case it is important that the party wall cavity seal follows the line of the insulation in the slope and horizontal ceiling sections (though for the purposes of Part B (Fire) it may be necessary to ensure that the fire cavity barrier follows the slope to the ridge). In the case of flats, the sealing system should follow the line of party floors and other party structures as well as the main thermal envelope.

5.7 In considering heat losses via party walls it is important to remember that wherever the wall penetrates an insulation layer, such as when the blockwork of a masonry party wall penetrates insulation at ceiling level, a thermal bridge is likely to exist. This will be the case even where the party wall U-value is zero. The evaluation of thermal bridges should ensure that any bridging at the party wall is taken into account along with other thermal bridges. It is important also to be satisfied that any solution to the party wall bypass does not contravene other parts of the Regulations, in particular Part E (Sound).

Table 3 **U-values for party walls**

Party wall construction	U-value (W/m²K)
Solid	0.0
Unfilled cavity with no effective edge sealing	0.5
Unfilled cavity with effective sealing around all exposed edges and in line with insulation layers in abutting elements	0.2
A fully filled cavity with effective sealing at all exposed edges and in line with insulation layers in abutting elements	0.0

5.8 The party wall is a particular case of the more general thermal bypass problem that occurs where the air barrier and the insulation layer are not contiguous and the cavity between them is subject to air movement. To avoid the consequent reduction in thermal performance, either the insulation layer should be contiguous with the air barrier at all points in the building envelope, or the space between them should be filled with solid material such as in a masonry wall.

Thermal bridges

5.9 The building fabric should be constructed so that there are no reasonably avoidable thermal bridges in the insulation layers caused by gaps within the various elements, at the joints between elements, and at the edges of elements such as those around window and door openings.

5.10 Where calculated in support of the approaches set out in paragraphs 5.12a and 5.12b, linear thermal transmittances and temperature factors should be calculated following the guidance set out in BR 497[16]. Reasonable provision would be to demonstrate that the specified details achieve a temperature factor that is no worse than the performance set out in BRE IP 1/06[17].

5.11 Similarly, in support of the approaches set out in paragraphs 5.12a and 5.12b, the builder would have to demonstrate that an appropriate system of site inspection is in place to give confidence that the construction procedures achieve the required standards of consistency.

5.12 Ways of demonstrating that reasonable provision has been made are:

a. To adopt a quality-assured accredited construction details approach in accordance with a scheme approved by the Secretary of State. If such a scheme is utilised then the calculated linear thermal transmittance can be used directly in the **DER** calculation;

For new buildings, such scheme(s) accredit and quality assure the calculation of the linear thermal transmittance, accredit details in terms of buildability and have an associated quality assurance regime that inspects a sample of sites to confirm that the details are being implemented correctly. The use of such schemes may also allow a reduction in the Building Control charges.

b. To use details that have not been subject to independent assessment of the construction method. However, in this case, the linear thermal transmittance should still have been calculated by a person with suitable expertise and experience following the guidance set out in BR 497, and a process flow sequence should be provided to the **BCB** indicating the way in which the detail should be constructed. The calculated value increased by 0.02 W/mK or 25 per cent whichever is greater can then be used in the **DER** calculation;

*Evidence of suitable expertise and experience for calculating linear thermal transmittance would be to demonstrate that the person has been trained in the software used to carry out the calculation, has applied that model to the example calculations set out in BR 497 and has achieved results that are within the stated tolerances. Builders following this route will inevitably add to the burden of checking required of the **BCB** and adopting this route may attract higher building control fees than the alternative approaches.*

c. To use unaccredited details, with no specific quantification of the thermal bridge values. In such cases a conservative default y-value of 0.15 must be used in the **DER** calculation.

5.13 The alternative approaches a and b above are not mutually exclusive. For example, a builder could use the accredited construction details scheme approach for the majority of the junctions, but use a bespoke detail for the window head. In this case, the 0.02 W/mK or 25 per cent, whichever is greater margin, would apply only to the thermal transmittance of the window head detail.

---

[16] BR 497 Conventions for calculating linear thermal transmittance and temperature factors, BRE 2007.
[17] IP 1/06 Assessing the effects of thermal bridging at junctions and around openings in the external elements of buildings, BRE 2006.

Air permeability and pressure testing

5.14   In order to demonstrate that an acceptable *air permeability* has been achieved, Regulation 20B states:

Pressure testing

20B.–(1) This regulation applies to the erection of a building in relation to which paragraph L1(a)(i) of Schedule 1 imposes a requirement.

(2) Where this regulation applies, the person carrying out the work shall, for the purpose of ensuring compliance with regulation 17C and paragraph L1(a)(i) of Schedule 1:

a. ensure that:

   i.   pressure testing is carried out in such circumstances as are approved by the Secretary of State; and

   ii. the testing is carried out in accordance with a procedure approved by the Secretary of State; and

b. subject to paragraph (5), give notice of the results of the testing to the local authority.

(3) The notice referred to in paragraph (2)(b) shall:

a. record the results and the data upon which they are based in a manner approved by the Secretary of State; and

b. be given to the local authority not later than seven days after the final test is carried out.

(4) A local authority is authorised to accept, as evidence that the requirements of paragraph (2)(a)(ii) have been satisfied, a certificate to that effect by a person who is registered by the British Institute of Non-destructive Testing in respect of pressure testing for the air tightness of buildings.

(5) Where such a certificate contains the information required by paragraph (3)(a), paragraph (2)(b) does not apply.

5.15   The approved procedure for pressure testing is given in the ATTMA publication *Measuring air permeability of building envelopes*[18], and, specifically, the method that tests the building envelope. The preferred test method is that trickle ventilators should be temporarily sealed rather than just closed. *BCBs* should be provided with evidence that test equipment has been calibrated within the previous 12 months using a UKAS-accredited facility. The manner approved for recording the results and the data on which they are based is given in section 4 of that document.

5.16   *BCBs* are authorised to accept, as evidence of compliance, a certificate offered under regulation 20B(4). It should be confirmed to the *BCB* that the person has received appropriate training and is registered to test the specific class of building concerned.

5.17   The approved circumstances under which the Secretary of State requires pressure testing to be carried out are set out in paragraphs 5.18 to 5.23.

5.18   On each development, an air pressure test should be carried out on three units of each *dwelling type* or 50 per cent of all instances of that *dwelling type*, whichever is the less. For the purposes of this Approved Document, a block of flats should be treated as a separate development irrespective of the number of blocks on the site. The *dwelling(s)* to be tested should be taken from the first completed batch of units of each *dwelling type*.

Most larger developments will include many dwelling types – and multiple units of each type should be tested to confirm the robustness of the designs and the construction procedures.

5.19   The specific *dwellings* making up the test sample should be selected by the *BCB* in consultation with the pressure tester. They should be selected so that about half of the scheduled tests for each *dwelling type* are carried out during construction of the first 25 per cent of each *dwelling type*. All tests on *dwellings* in the sample shall be reported to the *BCB*, including any test failure (see paragraphs 5.20 to 5.22).

The aim is to enable lessons to be learned and adjustments to design and/or site procedures to be made before the majority of the dwellings are built.

Showing compliance with regulation 20B and the consequences of failing a pressure test

5.20   Compliance with the requirements would be demonstrated if:

a. the measured *air permeability* is not worse than the limit value of 10 m³/(h.m²) at 50 Pa; and

b. the *DER* calculated using the measured *air permeability* is not worse than the *TER*.

This means that if a design adopted a low (i.e. better) design air permeability in order to achieve a performance better than the TER, it would not fail to comply with Part L if the pressure test achieved the limit value and the TER was achieved.

5.21   If satisfactory performance is not achieved, then remedial measures should be carried out on the *dwelling* and a new test carried out until the *dwelling* achieves the criteria set out in paragraph 5.20. In addition, a further *dwelling* of the same *dwelling type* should be tested, thereby increasing the overall sample size.

5.22   In addition to the remedial work on a *dwelling* that failed the initial test, other *dwellings* of the same *dwelling type* that have not been tested should be examined and, where appropriate, similar remedial measures applied.

---

[18]   Measuring air permeability in the envelopes of dwellings, Technical Standard L1, ATTMA, 2010

Alternative to pressure testing on small developments

5.23 As an alternative approach to specific pressure testing on development sites where no more than two **dwellings** are to be erected, reasonable provision would be:

a. to demonstrate that during the preceding 12 month period, a **dwelling** of the same **dwelling type** constructed by the same builder had been pressure tested according to the procedures given in paragraphs 5.14 to 5.19 and had achieved the **design air permeability**; or

b. avoid the need for any pressure testing by using a value of 15 m³/(h.m²) at 50 Pa for the **air permeability** when calculating the **DER**.

The effect of using this cautious value would then have to be compensated for by improved standards elsewhere in the dwelling design.

COMMISIONING OF HEATING AND HOT WATER SYSTEMS

5.24 Paragraph L1(b)(iii) of Schedule 1 to the Building Regulations requires **fixed building services** to be commissioned by testing and adjustment as necessary to ensure that they use no more fuel and power than is reasonable in the circumstances. In order to demonstrate that the heating and hot water systems have been adequately commissioned, regulation 20C states:

20C Commissioning

(A1) This regulation applies to building work in relation to which paragraph F1(2) of Schedule 1 imposes a requirement, but does not apply to the provision or extension of any fixed system for mechanical ventilation or any associated controls where testing and adjustment is not possible.

(1) This regulation applies to building work in relation to which paragraph L1(b) of Schedule 1 imposes a requirement, but does not apply to the provision or extension of any fixed building service where testing and adjustment is not possible or would not affect the energy efficiency of that fixed building service.

(2) Where this regulation applies the person carrying out the work shall, for the purpose of ensuring compliance with paragraph F1(2) or L1(b) of Schedule 1, give to the local authority a notice confirming that the fixed building services have been commissioned in accordance with a procedure approved by the Secretary of State.

(3) The notice shall be given to the local authority–

a. not later than the date on which the notice required by regulation 15(4) is required to be given; or

b. where that regulation does not apply, not more than 30 days after completion of the work.

5.25 It would be useful to prepare a commissioning plan, identifying the systems that need to be tested and the tests that will be carried out and provide this with the design stage **TER/DER** calculation so that the **BCB** can check the **commissioning** is being done as the work proceeds.

The use of the templates in the Model Commissioning Plan (BSRIA BG 8/2009) is a way of documenting the process in an appropriate way.

5.26 Not all **fixed building services** will need to be commissioned. With some systems adjustment is not possible as the only controls are 'on' and 'off' switches. Examples of this would be some mechanical extraction systems or single fixed electrical heaters. In other cases **commissioning** would be possible but in the specific circumstances would have no effect on energy use. **Fixed building services** which do not require **commissioning** should be identified in the commissioning plan, along with the reason for not requiring **commissioning**.

5.27 Where **commissioning** is carried out it must be done in accordance with a procedure approved by the Secretary of State. For heating and hot water systems the approved procedures are set out in the *Domestic building services compliance guide*. For ventilation systems, the approved procedure is set out in the *Domestic Ventilation: Installation and Commissioning Compliance Guide*[19].

5.28 **Commissioning** is often carried out by the person who installs the system. In other cases it may be carried out by a subcontractor or by a specialist firm. It is important that whoever carries it out follows the relevant approved procedure in doing so.

5.29 Where a building notice or full plans have been given to a local authority **BCB** the notice of completion of **commissioning** should be given to that **BCB** within five days of the completion of the **commissioning** work. In other cases, for example where work is carried out by a person registered with a competent person scheme (see paragraph 3.9), it must be given within 30 days.

5.30 Where an approved inspector is the **BCB** the notice of completion of **commissioning** should generally be given to the approved inspector within five days of the completion of work. However, where the work is carried out by a person registered with a competent person scheme (see paragraph 3.9) the notice must be given within 30 days. Where the installation of **fixed building services** which require **commissioning** is carried out by a person registered with a competent person scheme the notice of **commissioning** will be given by that person.

5.31 Until the **BCB** receives the commissioning notice it is likely that it cannot be reasonably satisfied that Part L has been complied with and consequently is unlikely to be able to give a completion/final certificate.

---

[19] Domestic Ventilation: Installation and Commissioning Compliance Guide, CLG, 2010.

Section 6: Providing information

CRITERION 5 – PROVISIONS FOR ENERGY-EFFICIENT OPERATION OF THE DWELLING

6.1 In accordance with paragraph L1(c) of Schedule 1, the owner of the *dwelling* should be provided with sufficient information about the building, the *fixed building services* and their maintenance requirements so that the building can be operated in such a manner as to use no more fuel and power than is reasonable in the circumstances.

6.2 A way of complying with the requirement would be to provide a suitable set of operating and maintenance instructions aimed at achieving efficiency in the use of fuel and power in a way that householders can understand, in a durable format that can be kept and referred to over the service life of the system(s). The instructions should be directly related to the particular system(s) installed in the *dwelling*.

6.3 Without prejudice to the need to comply with health and safety requirements, the instructions should explain to the occupier of the *dwelling* how to operate the system(s) efficiently. This should include:

a. how to make adjustments to the timing and temperature control settings; and

b. what routine maintenance is needed to enable operating efficiency to be maintained at a reasonable level through the service live(s) of the system(s).

6.4 The data used to calculate the *TER* and the *DER* should be included with the operating and maintenance instructions. The occupier should also be provided with the recommendations report generated in parallel with the 'on-construction' Energy Performance Certificate. This will inform the occupier how the energy performance of the *dwelling* might be further improved.

It would also be sensible to retain an electronic copy of the TER/DER input file for the energy calculation to facilitate any future analysis that may be required by the owner when altering or improving the building.

Section 7: Model designs

7.1   Some builders may prefer to adopt model design packages rather than to engage in design for themselves. These model packages of fabric U-values, boiler seasonal efficiencies, window opening allowances, etc. should achieve compliant overall performance within certain constraints. The construction industry may develop model designs for this purpose, with information about such designs being made available at www.modeldesigns.info

7.2   It will still be necessary to demonstrate compliance in the particular case by going through the procedures described in paragraphs 4.7 to 4.14.

Appendix A: Reporting evidence of compliance

1. To facilitate effective communication between the builder and **BCB**, it would be beneficial to adopt a standardised format for presenting the evidence that demonstrates compliance with the **energy efficiency requirements**. (Other than the CO_2 target, which is mandatory, the other compliance criteria represent reasonable provision in normal circumstances. In unusual circumstances, alternative limits may represent reasonable provision, but this would have to be demonstrated in the particular case.)

2. Since the data in SAP 2009 and the results they calculate can provide a substantial proportion of the evidence in support of the compliance demonstration, it is anticipated that software implementations of SAP 2009 will produce this report as a standard output option.

3. It is anticipated that two versions of the standardised report would be produced by software implementations of SAP 2009: the first before commencement of works to include the **TER/DER** calculation plus supporting list of specifications and the second after completion to include the as built **TER/DER** calculation plus any changes to the list of specifications. The first design-stage report and accompanying list of specifications can then be used by the **BCB** to assist checking that what has been designed is actually built. A standardised report should enable the source of the evidence to be indicated, and allow the credentials of those submitting the evidence to be declared.

4. An important part of demonstrating compliance is to make a clear connection between the product specifications and the data inputs required by the compliance software (e.g. what is the wall construction that delivers the claimed U-value?). Examples as to how compliance software might provide this link are:

a. By giving each data input a reference code that can be mapped against a separate submission by the builder/developer that details the specification corresponding to each unique reference code in the data input.

b. By providing a fee-text entry facility along with each input parameter that has a unique reference code, thereby allowing the software to capture the specification of each item and so include the full details in an integrated output report.

c. By including one or more utility programs that derive the data input from the specification, e.g. a U-value calculator that conforms to BR 443 and that calculates the U-value based on the layer thicknesses and conductivities, repeating thermal bridge effects etc. Outputs from such a utility program could then automatically generate the type of integrated report described at b. above.

It would also help the **BCB** if the software included a facility to compare the 'as designed' and 'as constructed' data input files and automatically produce a schedule of changes.

5. The report should highlight any items whose specification is better than typically expected values. The **BCB** can then give particular attention to such 'key features', as their appropriate installation will be critical in achieving the **TER**. The **BCB** should give particular attention to those aspects where the claimed specification delivers an energy efficiency standard in advance of that defined in the following schedule.

Parameter	
Wall U-value	0.20 W/m²K
Roof U-value	0.13 W/m²K
Floor U-value	0.20 W/m²K
Window/door U-value	1.50 W/m²K
Party wall U-value	0.20 W/m²K
Thermal bridging value	0.04 W/m²K
Design air permeability	5.0 m³/(h.m²) at 50 Pa
Any secondary heating appliance	
Any item involving SAP Appendix Q	
Use of any low carbon or renewable energy technology	

Note: Solutions using electric resistance heating may have to better several of these fabric parameters if the design does not include an element of renewable energy provision.

Appendix B: Documents referred to

Air Tightness Testing and Measurement Association (ATTMA)

www.attma.org

Measuring air permeability in the air envelopes of dwellings, Technical Standard L1, 2010.

BRE

www.bre.co.uk

BR 443 Conventions for U-value calculations, 2006. (Available at www.bre.co.uk/uvalues)

Information Paper IP1/06 *Assessing the effects of thermal bridging at junctions and around openings in the external elements of buildings*, 2006. ISBN 978 1 86081 904 9

BRE Report BR 497 *Conventions for Calculating Linear Thermal Transmittance and Temperature Factors* 2007. ISBN 978 1 86081 986 5

BSRIA

www.bsria.co.uk

BSRIA BG 8/2009 Model Commissioning Plan

CIBSE

www.cibse.org

TM 36 Climate change and the indoor environment: impacts and adaptation, 2005. ISBN 978 1 90328 750 7

Department for Business, Innovation and Skills

www.bis.gov.uk

Technical Standards and Regulations Directive 98/34/EC (Available at: www.bis.gov.uk/policies/innovation/infrastructure/standardisation/tech-standards-directive)

Department for Energy and Climate Change (DECC)

www.decc.gov.uk

The Government's Standard Assessment Procedure for energy rating of dwellings, SAP 2009. (Available at www.bre.co.uk/sap2009)

SEDBUK Boiler Efficiency Database (Available at www.sedbuk.com)

Department for Communities and Local Government

www.communities.gov.uk

Notice of Approval of the methodology of calculation of the energy performance of buildings in England and Wales

Planning Policy Statement Planning and Climate Change (Available to download from: www.communities.gov.uk/planningandbuilding/planning/planningpolicyguidance/planningpolicystatements/planningpolicystatements/ppsclimatechange/)

Health and Safety Executive (HSE)

www.hse.gov.uk

L24 Workplace Health, Safety and Welfare: Workplace (Health, Safety and Welfare) Regulations1992, Approved Code of Practice and Guidance.

NBS (on behalf of Communities and Local Government)

www.thebuildingregs.com

Domestic Building Services Compliance Guide, CLG, 2010.

Domestic Ventilation Compliance Guide, CLG, 2010.

(Both available to download from: http://www.planningportal.gov.uk.)

Legislation

SI 1991/1620 Construction Products Regulations 1991

SI 1994/3051 Construction Products (Amendment) Regulations 1994

SI 1994/3260 Electrical Equipment (Safety) Regulations 1994

SI 2000/2532 The Building (Approved Inspectors etc.) Regulations 2000

SI 2007/991 Energy Performance of Buildings (Certificates and Inspections) (England and Wales) Regulations 2007

As implemented by the Electromagnetic Compatibility Regulations 2006 (SI 2006/3418)

Decision No 1/95 of the EC-Turkey Association Council of 22 December 1995

Appendix C: Standards referred to

BS EN ISO 13370:2007 Thermal performance of buildings. Heat transfer via the ground. Calculation methods.

BS 8206-2:2008 Lighting for buildings. Code of practice for daylighting.

BS EN 14351-1:2006 Windows and doors. Product standard, performance characteristics. Windows and external pedestrian doorsets without resistance to fire and/or smoke leakage characteristics.

A

Accredited construction details schemes 5.12–5.13
Air permeability 4.8
  Definitions 3.1
  Fabric standards Table 2
  Testing 5.14–5.23
Approved Document L1A
  Conventions 1.9
  Purpose 1.1–1.6
  Types of work covered 3.2–3.5
Assessed air permeability 3.1, 4.8
Asset rating 4.1
Attic rooms 5.6

B

BCB
  See Building Control Body (BCB)
Boiler efficiency 4.11
British Standards Appendix C
  BS 8206–2: 2008 4.27
  BS EN 14351-1 4.21
  BS EN ISO 13370 3.33
Building Control Body (BCB)
  Air permeability test results 5.15–5.16, 5.19
  Definition 3.1
  Demonstrating compliance 3.24–3.34, 4.9–4.11, Appendix A
  Notice of completion of commissioning 5.29–5.31
  Notification of work 3.7–3.10, 4.10
Building fabric
  Construction quality 5.2–5.13
  Design flexibility 4.18–4.19
  U-values 4.20–4.22, Table 2
Building log book 6.2–6.4
Building Regulations 2.1
Building services
  See Fixed building services

C

Cavity walls 5.3–5.8, Table 3,
CE marking 3.14
Certification
  Competent person self-certification schemes 3.7–3.12
  Product certification schemes 3.16–3.18
Chimneys 4.12
CO_2 emission rate
  See Dwelling CO_2 Emission Rate (DER); Target CO_2 Emission Rate (TER)
Commissioning
  Definition 3.1
  Heating and hot water systems 5.24–5.31
Common areas 3.31
Community energy systems 4.16
Competent person self-certification schemes 3.7–3.12
Compliance with requirements 1.2–1.3, 1.11
  Demonstrating 3.24–3.34, 4.9–4.11, Appendix A
  Materials and workmanship 3.14, 3.18
  Self-certification 3.10
Condensation risk 4.22
Conservatories 3.32
Construction quality 5.1–5.23
Controlled fittings 3.1
  See also Doors; Windows

Controlled services 3.1
  See also Fixed building services

D

Daylighting 4.27
DER
  See Dwelling CO_2 Emission Rate (DER)
Design air permeability 3.1
Design flexibility 3.26, 4.15, 4.18–4.19
Design standards 4.1–4.27
Doors Table 2
Dwelling
  Definition 3.1
Dwelling CO_2 Emission Rate (DER) 3.25, 3.28
  Calculation 4.7–4.8, 4.9–4.11
  Internal lighting 4.13
  Multiple dwellings 4.14
  Secondary heating 4.12
  Construction consistent with 5.1
  Definition 3.1
Dwelling type
  Definition 3.1

E

Emission Factor Adjustment (EFA) 4.4
Energy assessors 4.9
Energy efficiency requirements 2.1
  Compliance with 1.2–1.3, 1.11
  Definition 3.1
  Fixed building services 4.23–4.24
Energy performance
  Calculation 4.1
  Minimum requirements 4.1–4.2
  See also Dwelling CO_2 Emission Rate (DER); Target CO_2 Emission Rate (TER)
Energy Performance Certificate 2.1, 6.4
European Technical Approval 3.14, 3.21
Exemptions 3.6

F

Fabric
  See Building fabric
Fixed building services
  Commissioning 5.24–5.31
  Definition 3.1
  Limits on design flexibility 3.26, 4.18–4.19
  System efficiencies 4.23–4.24
Floors Table 2
Flues 4.12
Fuel factor Table 1, 4.4–4.5

G

Gas fires 4.12
Glazing 4.21–4.22, Table 2

H

Health and safety 3.23
Heating and hot water systems
  Commissioning 5.24–5.31
  Multiple systems 4.12, 4.17
  See also Fixed building services

I

Information provision 6.1–6.4
Internal lighting 4.13

L

Legislation Appendix B
  European 3.14
  See also Building Regulations
Lighting 4.13
Limitation on requirements 2.2–2.3
Limiting air permeability 3.1
Live-work units 3.3
Low and zero carbon (LZC) technologies 4.15, 4.17
Low-energy lighting 4.13

M

Maintenance instructions 6.2–6.4
Material change of use 3.5
Materials and workmanship 3.13–3.22
Minimum energy performance requirements 4.1–4.2
Mixed-use buildings 3.4
Model designs 7.1–7.2
Multiple dwellings 3.31, 4.6, 4.14
Multiple heating systems 4.12, 4.17

N

Notice of completion of commissioning 5.29–5.31
Notification of work 3.7–3.12

O

Open fires 4.12
Operating and maintenance instructions 6.2–6.4
Operational rating 4.1

P

Party walls 5.3–5.8
  Energy performance calculation 4.4
  U-values 5.5–5.7, Table 2, Table 3
Passive control measures 3.27, 4.25
Porches 3.32
Pressure testing 5.14–5.22
Product certification schemes 3.16–3.18
Publications (excluding BSI and European Standards) Appendix B
  Assessing the effects of thermal bridging at junctions and around openings in the external elements of buildings (BRE IP 1/06, 2008) 5.10
  Climate change and the indoor environment (CIBSE TM 36, 2005) 4.26
  Construction Products Regulations 1991 (SI 1991/1620) 3.14
  Conventions for calculating linear thermal transmittance and temperature factors (BRE 497, 2007) 5.10
  Conventions for U-value calculations (BR 443, 2006) 4.21
  Domestic Building Services Compliance Guide (CLG, 2010) 4.23–4.24
  Electrical Equipment (Safety) Regulations 1994 (SI 1994/3260) 3.14
  Electromagnetic Compatibility Regulations 2006 (SI 2006/3418) 3.14
  Measuring air permeability of building envelopes (Technical Standard L1,

ATTMA, 2010) 5.15
Model Commissioning Plan (BSRIA
BG 8/2009) 5.25

Q

Quality assurance 5.1–5.23

R

Rooflights 4.22
Roofs Table 2
Roof windows 4.22, Table 2
Room for residential purposes
    Definition 3.1

S

SAP 2009 Appendix A (2–3), 3.24,
    4.3–4.5, 4.26
Secondary heating 4.12
Self-certification schemes 3.7–3.12
Software Appendix A(2–4)
Solar control 3.27, 4.25–4.27
Solar hot water systems 4.17
Special areas 3.30–3.34
Standard Assessment Procedure
    See SAP 2009
Standards 3.19–3.22
    See also British Standards
Swimming pools 3.33–3.34
System efficiencies 4.23–4.24

T

Target CO$_2$ Emission Rate (TER) 3.25,
    3.28, 4.2–4.5
    Calculation 4.3–4.4, 4.6
    Definition 3.1
    Multiple dwellings 4.6
Technical specifications 3.19–3.22
Thermal bridges 5.7–5.13
Thermal elements
    See Building fabric
Trade-offs 3.26, 4.13

U

U-values 4.21–4.22, Table 2

W

Walls Table 2, Table 3
Windows 4.21–4.22, Table 2
Workmanship 3.13–3.22
**Workplace (Health, Safety and
    Welfare) Regulations 1992** 3.23

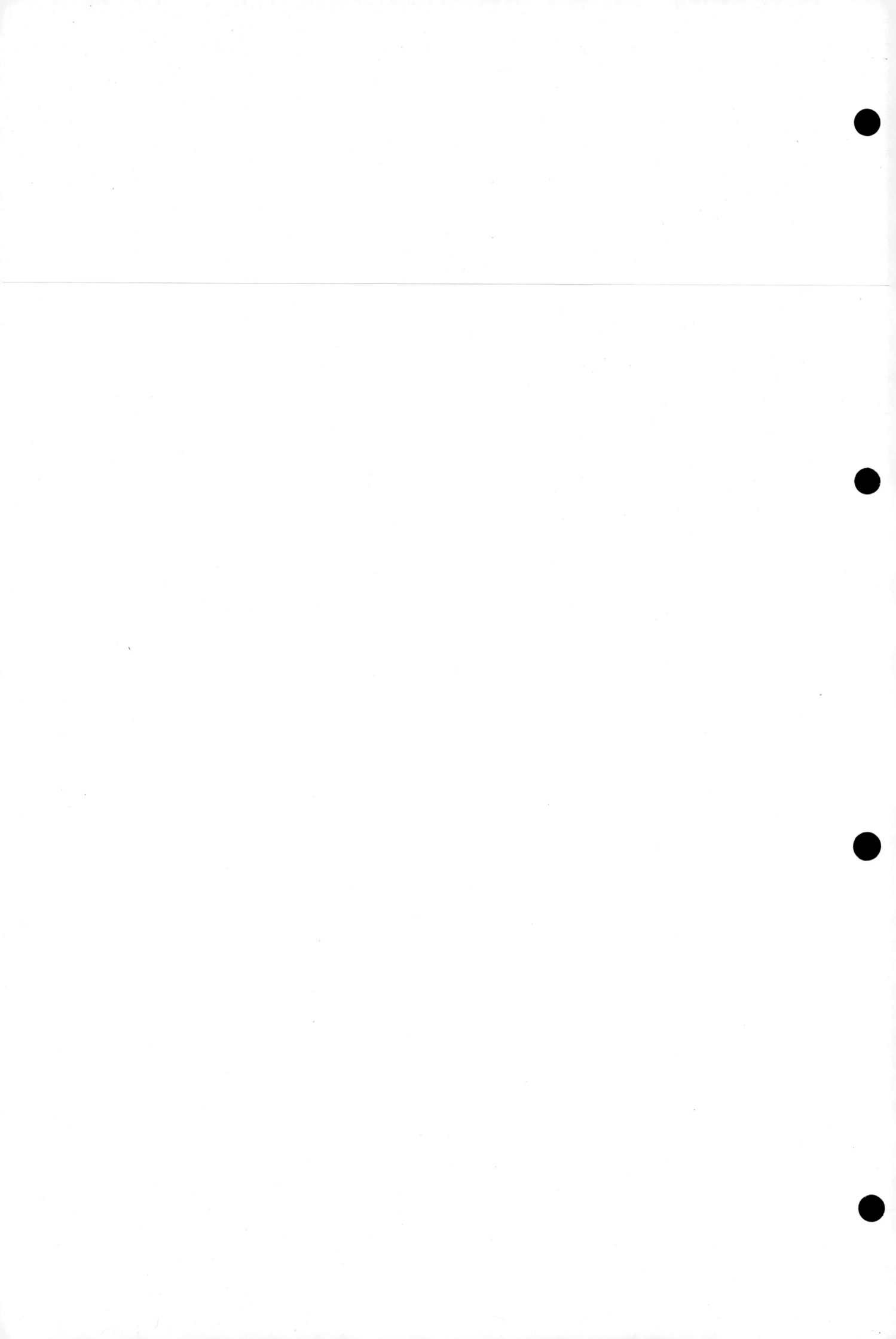